Tropical Colors

Tropical Colors

The Art of Living with Tropical Flowers

Sakul Intakul and Wongvipa Devahastin na Ayudhya

With Peta Bassett

Photographs by Luca Invernizzi Tettoni

PERIPLUS

Published by Periplus Editions (HK) Ltd

Copyright © 2002 Periplus Editions (HK) Ltd
Text © 2002 Sakul Intakul
and Wongvipa Devahastin na Ayudhya
Photos © 2002 Luca Invernizzi Tettoni

Distributed by:
North America, Latin America and Europe
Tuttle Publishing,
364 Innovation Drive,
North Clarendon, VT 05759-9436, USA
Tel (802) 773 8930; fax (802) 773 6993
Email: info@tuttlepublishing.com
www.tuttlepublishing.com

Asia Pacific
Berkeley Books Pte Ltd, 130 Joo Seng Road
#06-01/03, Singapore 368357
Tel (65) 6280 1330; fax (65) 6280 6290
Email: inquiries@periplus.com.sg
www.periplus.com

Japan
Tuttle Publishing, Yaekari Building, 3F,
5-4-12 Osaki, Shinagawa-ku,
Tokyo 141-0032
Tel (03) 5437 0171; fax (03) 5437 0755
Email: tuttle-sales@gol.com

ISBN 0 7946 0056 5

Design: mind, London

Printed in Singapore

09 08 07 06 05
 7   6   5   4   3

Front cover: Globe amaranth stems
float in a mesh of fine copper wire.
Half title page: A platform of pandanus
leaves supports a miniature cattleya.
Title page: Suspended pink curcumas
rise towards floating candles. *This
page:* Mauve-pink miniature cattleyas
supported on bamboo skewers add
color to folded pandanus leaves.

CONTENTS

INTRODUCTION

Flowers have always been an integral part of the cultural fabric of Thailand and a constant reminder of the country's Buddhist heritage and identity. They are indispensable in age-old acts of worship and play an important role in festivals and celebrations. Flowers are also woven into the daily lives of the people. Venerated Buddha images in temples throughout the country are cloaked in floral offerings. On their way to work, many Thais offer *malai* (garlands) and heartfelt prayers at wayside shrines. Taxi and *tuk-tuk* (auto-rickshaw) drivers regularly adorn their rear vision mirrors with strings of fragrant blossoms. *Malai* are also given in greeting.

The abundance of flowers available from Thailand's markets and street stalls is a reflection of the wealth and diversity of its tropical environment. The country's long rainy season, during which both the temperature and humidity drop considerably, followed by a lengthy dry spell, contribute to the variety: lush, moisture-loving plants growing with abandon almost anywhere vie for attention with spectacular flowering trees which need a prolonged dry season to bloom. Although different conditions foster different plant environments, the more than 200,000 species native to countries that straddle

the equater and nearby subtropical regions are all the result of abundant sun and moisture. All offer a rich source of inspiration with which to create memorable floral arrangements.

A steady movement of plants around the tropical world has given gardeners and florists alike access to an immense array of plant material. A private garden in Bali, for instance, is likely to offer an international display – heliconias from South America, frangipanis from Central America, bougainvilleas from Brazil, flamboyant trees from Madagascar, anthuriums from the West Indies, red gingers from Malaysia – all of them growing with the vigor of native plants. Commercial production of tropical plants and faster transportation has also meant that many plants grown in tropical regions are now available as cut flowers in the West, albeit at a price.

Westerners have long been fascinated with tropical plants, a direct result of the epic voyages of early explorers in search of new lands and rare spices. Their tales of the tropics and an "eternal spring" were undoubtedly met with disbelief when they returned from the New World. Long skirts dragged over moss-covered walkways and spectacles fogged over in the hothouses of Europe where people flocked to witness for

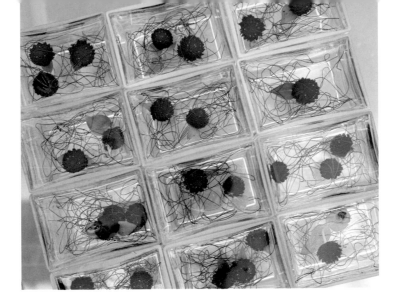

Left: Distinctive lotus seed pods provide textural contrast on a panel of ribbed banana leaves.

Right: The fine green stems and leaves of the purple globe amaranth complement the fine copper mesh in this glass grid arrangement.

Below right: Horsetail stems pierced by bamboo skewers form platforms for white curcuma bracts.

themselves the imported vibrancy and rare exotic forms on display. For most tropical plants, their introduction into glass-houses that approximated tropical conditions was the first step towards hybridization and eventual acclaim as house plants. Over the years, the varieties that have returned to the tropics are often quite different from the original, contributing further to the diversity.

As bewitching as many tropical blooms may appear, their very nature is also intriguing. What seem to be pale petals on the musseanda tree are, in fact, decorative leaves. The scooped protrusions of the heliconia are actually exten-sions of the leaves or bract while the true flower remains hidden. The way in which some tropical plant life is propa-gated is also curious. The bird of paradise, native to South Africa, is pollinated by sunbirds which are attracted to its orange sepals. After having their fill of nectar, they fly on to the next plant with pollen on their feet. Other flowers, including gardenias and tuberoses, are white and release heady scents at night to attract specific insects. Mystique surrounds tropi-cal flora and is yet another alluring feature of its appeal.

Flowers, however, are not the sole fascination of the tropics. Leaves and stems command attention in their own right, whether in starring or supporting roles. The seemingly endless variety of striking shapes, sizes and colors, as well as texture, all contribute to a rich collage of design potential.

Left: Bunches of plump lotus buds wrapped in their own waxy leaves are a common sight at Pak Klong Talad, Bangkok's bustling flower market.

Right: Bold bracts of red and yellow *Heliconia caribeae* held upright by golden bamboo frames make a dramatic display in this contemporary interior.

Tropical Colors: The Art of Living with Tropical Flowers demonstrates how the vast palette of tropical flowers and foliage can be used to create innovative floral designs for contemporary spaces, both indoor and out. Techniques vary from single stem arrangements to floating water installations and conceptual Buddhist-inspired works in which soaring brass frames cradle reeds, lotuses and tuberoses. Although the designs in this book were created and realized in Bangkok, the flora used can be found in all corners of the tropical world – as well as in florists' refrigerators in the West. Similarly, technique and inspiration are drawn from the diverse cultures surrounding the equator. Capturing the context of tropical life is as integral to floral design as the foliage itself.

Tropical Colors elevates flowers beyond the realm of common and casual applications. The designs exhibit a raw industrial edge that reveals Sakul Intakul's early training as an engineer. Others draw on the floral artist's abiding interest in Buddhism. Most of the arrangements are, in fact, sculptures: multi-dimensional works, both physically and conceptually, that can be appreciated from a number of angles.

The use of unconventional supporting materials, such as cages and webs of chicken wire and contorted bundles of fine copper wire, is another hallmark of the arrangements in this book. They add defining lines, rhythm, punctuation and a novel approach that can be readily replicated in any home,

irrespective of latitude. Equally surprising is the role of stems and leaves that contribute their color and texture to compositions throughout and which are also assembled into innovative supporting structures.

The unifying thread running through the floral arrangements in *Tropical Colors* is respect for the individual bloom. To this end, the astonishing bracts of the curcuma and the waxy petals of orchids are revealed in elegant submerged arrangements. The delicate fragility of hibiscus blooms is framed in floating designs. The synthetic looking spathes of anthuriums and the voluptuous forms of cattleyas are highlighted when placed against lush leaf coils, while the dramatic colors and shapes of heliconias are accentuated in bamboo scaffolds. Each arrangement strikes a balance between the flora, the form of the arrangement and the built environment. Distinctive compositions are as sensitive to their locations as they are to the dynamic between the elements within.

Tropical Colors: The Art of Living with Tropical Flowers is an invitation to experiment with tropical flowers and foliage or, if these are not available, suitable temperate plants. Almost any blossom can be set afloat in a contemplative centerpiece, both indoors and out. Whether you are curled up on a sunny daybed for a leisurely afternoon read or reaching for last-minute ideas for a table setting before guests arrive, be inspired to explore new dimensions in floral design.

UNDERWATER ALLURE

New territory is being explored in tropical floral art as water is elevated from a life-sustaining element to a display medium. Blooms and foliage are plunged below the waterline in translucent vessels, revealing another dimension in floral creativity, one that can be appreciated from a multitude of angles. The resulting dynamic offers simple floral solutions for any space, from large public installations to intimate table settings. Subtle reflections of the subjects within, whether a riotous glory lily or the understated crown flower, provide a delicate interplay of light and color with the surroundings. Further appeal, and an element of surprise, is added by the mist-like pockets of air trapped in the fine filaments of leaves and flowers.

TANK ART

Single tropical blooms suspended by wire and anchored by stones in large acrylic or glass vessels can make a dramatic statement in any home. The texture and thickness of a flower determines its suitability for submersion. Flowers and stems with thick, waxy petals that are not easily bruised are ideal, though experimentation is recommended. Composition is as vital below the waterline as it is above. Space is the key. A rhythmic use of voids in and around a flower can magnify its presence, whereas overcrowding may literally drown it. Balance, movement, line and repetition should all be considered when creating a harmonious yet distinctive display.

Left: Rims of fire appear to float above the black granite flooring in this dramatic entranceway. Top–down lighting illuminates the pebble-lined bases of the custom-designed acrylic tanks in which tiny pink curcuma rise up to meet floating candles. Reflections from the glass-lined corridor magnify the effect of a gallery space.

Opposite: Floor-to-ceiling windows reinforce the feeling of translucency that flows throughout Raymond Eaton's home. The central courtyard pool further merges interior and exterior boundaries, while flickering candles float above elegant curcuma stems and lend an air of intimacy to the grand scale of the setting.

Stainless steel tubing appears to be freestanding in this arrangement placed in a sandstone niche. Intensely colored cattleya blooms peer out from the metallic folds which, along with the curved line of the phormium leaf, are inspired by the Japanese *obi* (sash).

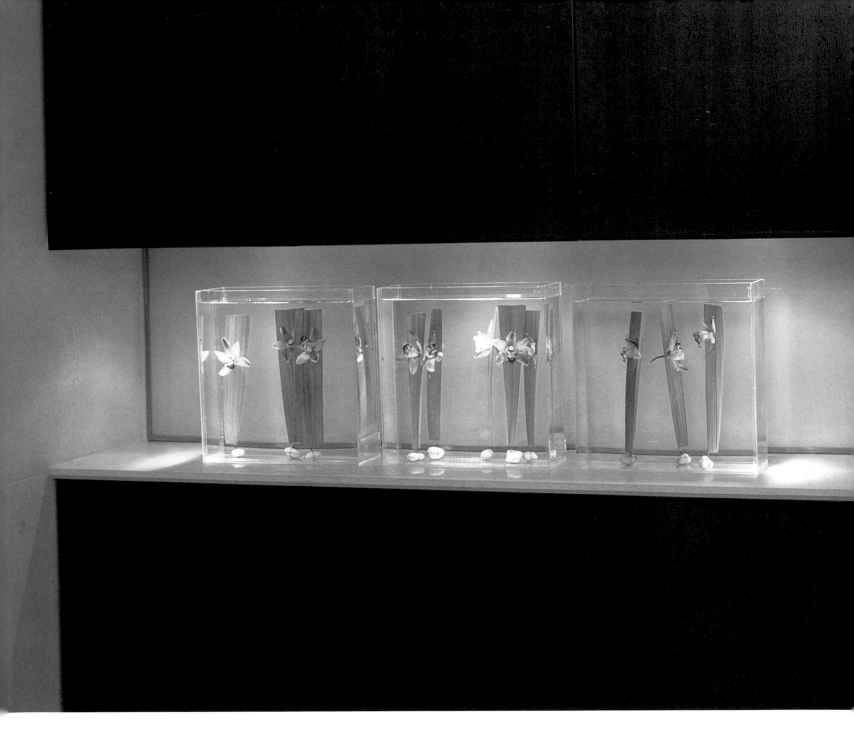

A welcoming committee of
trimmed orchid leaves pierced
by miniature green cymbidiums
stands to attention in an
understated entrance hall. The
flowers are fastened at the
back of the spathoglotis leaves
with pins. The floating leaves
are anchored with stones.

IN UNISON

Water is a voluminous frame that elevates even the most generic blossom to exhibition status. Detached but not disconnected, the repetition of the same bloom across an array of identical vessels creates an effortless formality and rhythm that flows in and around the entire arrangement. While order is imposed on the flowers, the result is far from monotonous as subtle variations are revealed and differing heights add movement to the overall composition. The containers remain plain and standardized so as not to compete with the subjects within. The subtle play of light and color adds further intrigue to each stem, secure in its own watery world.

Left: Boundaries blur as a rhythmic line of pink curcuma, also known as Siamese tulips, appear to emerge from the watery depths. The varied heights and positions of the bracts add to this illusion.

Right: The reptilian form of the bracts of *Tillandsia cyanea*, commonly called pink quill, gently spinning on their axes, contrasts with the cylindrical vases and tubular table frame. The lime to pink transition offsets the atmospheric hues of the surrounding surfaces.

Angelfish make a dramatic and dynamic addition to this linear array of green and white curcuma. This is not only a stunning decorative idea but will, no doubt, be a talking point when entertaining. The fish, of course, need to be returned to their permanent and, hopefully, larger home when your guests leave. The arrangement is easily replicated using other tropical plants and fish.

Creating a strong sense of procession, submerged glory lilies lead to the inner sanctums of this home. Encased in round glass bowls, the vivid red, yellow and lime flame-shaped petals are a perfect complement to the black granite flooring below. Each flower is anchored with wire to a beautiful white river stone, providing further color contrast.

Encased in an orderly display
of glass, these glory lilies
at first appear to be identical.
Closer inspection, however,
reveals the age of each bloom:
lime green centers emerge
from younger flowers while
a deep reddish-orange hue
suffuses older neighbors.

SUNKEN TREASURES

Lending a metallic edge to modern floral design, two utilitarian products normally associated with industrial applications have entered the realm of aesthetics. Coiled copper wire and standard mesh wire not only make innovative and unusual supporting materials for what is essentially a feminine subject, but also inject an elemental contrast with the surrounding water. Malleable copper takes on a form of its own when shaped and massed below the surface, anchoring and gilding delicate blooms. Mesh wire is transformed into elegant, reusable weights that not only protect the precious blooms within but provide an alluring framework.

Left: Purple crown flowers are entwined in this aqueous copper wire nest. The fluidity of the floral arrangement is in stark contrast to the structured lines of the adjacent wire frame chair, table and lampstand. The irregular surface detail on the glass container provides its own twist to the design.

Right: The varied density of the contorted wire adds another dimension to the arrangement. Crown flowers can be substituted with other suitable blooms in toning or contrasting colors.

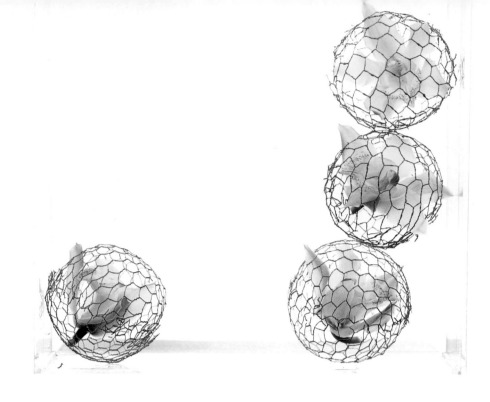

Left: Not normally appreciated for its aesthetic value, chicken wire is used to both frame and anchor these cymbidiums in a honeycomb lattice. Placed inside a water-filled acrylic container, the floral "frames" merge harmoniously with their watery surroundings.

Below: Stems of the purple globe amaranth – "flowers that never wither" – are casually placed inside wire-filled glass containers in this modern sideboard arrangement.

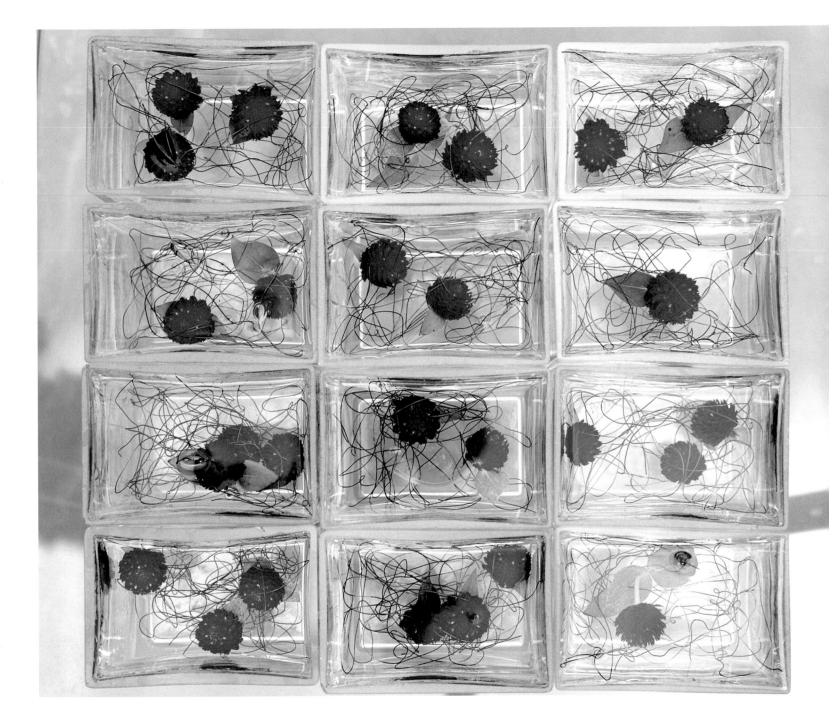

The fine stems and leaves of
the purple globe amaranth add
a dash of lime to this glass grid
arrangement. Masses of tiny
air bubbles combine with the
coiled copper wire to produce
an effervescent effect.

STILL WATERS

Water is a conduit for tropical life. Floating markets carry trade. Homes on stilts support entire communities. Canals irrigate orchards and ricefields, and from the ocean comes the catch of the day. Floating arrangements conjure up images of lotus-filled ponds, of young seedlings emerging from flooded rice paddies, or the meandering path of a fallen leaf journeying downstream. The simple act of floating flowers in anticipation of arriving guests or for personal pleasure can have both a cleansing and calming effect. Floating arrangements are also suited to the ephemeral nature of tropical flowers. Many do not last long once cut, but it is easy to create and replenish these enchanting floating arrangements with each new day.

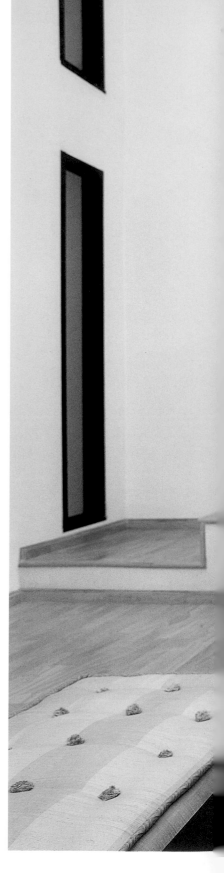

MASSED MAGIC

Simple, stylish and contemporary, a mass of floating blooms free of their foliage makes a dramatic statement in any space, be it an entranceway, a living room or a courtyard setting. This is an effective way to inject a splash of color into a room of muted hues or to highlight those already present in the surrounding décor. Container sizes for floating arrangements can vary from teacups to swimming pools, although the effect of a motionless watery canvas is more easily achieved in small, shallow vessels. Both long-lasting flowers such as the orchid and short-lived blooms such as the hibiscus are suitable. The latter can be replenished daily from the garden.

Above and right: Resting in a water-filled tray, star-shaped mokara add the final touch to this exotic canvas of mauve and fuschia vanda orchids and reddish-yellow miniature cattleya hybrids. Framed by the generous tabletop in designer Ou Baholydhin's Bangkok living room, this eye-catching display concentrates the colors of the surroundings.

Left and right: Under watchful eyes, the rich purple and yellow hues of water lilies welcome guests into the home of Velvadi Sritrairatana and her husband, interior designer Viboon Techakalayatum. In the calm of this muted foyer, the lilies, floating in a large hand-beaten stainless steel tray, tease their admirers by opening and closing in response to changes in light throughout the day.

TRANQUIL NOTES

Delicate blossoms afloat in a ceramic container create a mood of contemplation and sensuality. Waking to a fragrant frangipani floating in a dainty porcelain bowl can set the tone for the day ahead. Taking the time to create or simply to view such simple gestures can have a calming effect. Composition is easy. All that is required are a number of freshly picked blooms from your garden and a sharp pair of scissors with which to trim the stems daily when replacing the water. Limiting flowers to the one variety usually works best in small bowls, which can then be placed on tables, on the ground around indoor pools or along walkways.

Above: Fragrant *Wrightia religiosa* blossoms encircle the bases of bronze Sakul Intakul "chedi" vessels. From the center rises the mythical Mount Meru, the Buddhist and Hindu spiritual center of the universe.

Right: This small hand-thrown ceramic bowl reflects the scale of the floating lantana flowers, at the same time providing a miniature contemplation feature.

PASSING PARADES

Courtyard water features, dark reflection ponds and even swimming pools can form a sophisticated canvas for larger floating arrangements. The intrinsic charm of flowers adrift lies in their unpredictability as "floral happenings". They take on a life of their own, unfolding at whim and evolving in response to subtle changes in the surrounding environment. To ensure that the impact of the flowers is not diluted given the scale of the setting, simple structural details can be added – banana trunk rings and rolled leaves act as flotation devices, while coconut frond skewers secure flowers to leaves and add form and line to the overall arrangement.

Below and right: Two varieties of both "ti" plant leaves and desert roses are set adrift in a calm water feature. The rolled leaves, secured with coconut frond spines, are evocative of vernacular watercraft. Their colors complement their delicate floral subjects.

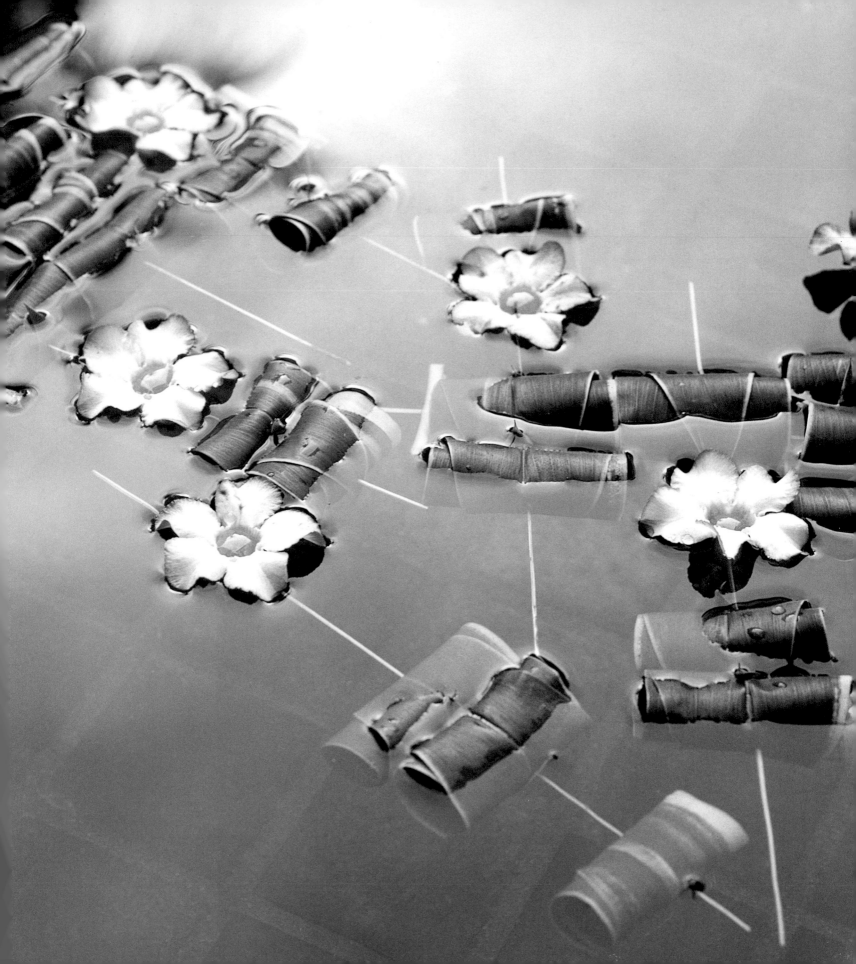

Ivory and green-tinged rings from the trunk of a banana plant form an innovative platform for this floral arrangement. Pink hibiscus blossoms rest upon the floral floats in tranquil repose, while flickering candles inserted into the center of the banana rings add a romantic touch. Bamboo skewers connect each ring in a loose and flowing formation that retains a semblance of order.

FLORAL CROSSINGS

An oasis of calm within a modern cityscape is a rare and precious find, one in which floral arrangements need to be carefully introduced so as not to disrupt the existing ambience. Armfuls of brilliant green stems can be tamed into floating bridges or rafts, dotted with boldly colored exotic blooms. Free of foliage, they take on the appearance of vivid brushstrokes. Plastic thread is used to connect the stems and maintain the form of the rafts. A flower as rich in symbolism as the water lily makes an ideal contrast to the modern, almost minimalist feel of linear flower stems. Such "suspended illusions" can be created in any tranquil indoor or out-door pond, though scale and proportion need to be considered.

Right and opposite: "Bridges" of vibrant green water hyacinth stems connected by invisible threads and sprinkled with dazzling yellow water lilies stretch across the tranquil, *chedi*-lined inner courtyard pond at The Sukhothai Bangkok. The stems of the water lilies reach through the platforms to drink from the pond below. Both stems and lilies combine to infuse warm tropical color into a restrained yet reverent setting.

FOLIAGE IN FOCUS

Tropical environments are notable for the extravagance of their vegetation: broad, paddle-shaped leaves, vast swags of climbers hanging from trees, a multitude of palms and ferns and the ubiquitous bamboo. Although tropical flowers are more likely to take center stage – the brilliant spectrum of bougainvilleas, the alien forms of orchids, the bewitching line of the bird of paradise and the eternal charm of the lotus are hard to ignore – leaves are dramatic elements in their own right. The line, shape, texture and vibrancy of tropical leaves offer a wealth of exotic inspiration and can give structure and context to a floral arrangement. If the right container is not available, you need only look to tropical foliage for support.

Left: Rolled blue flax lily leaves placed in water-filled handmade teak trays complement the strong lines and neutral tones of this interior. *Nerium oleander* flowers rest atop the leaves which have been rolled alternately with their fronts and backs exposed.

Right: A cylindrical acrylic vessel holds coils of interlinked coconut fronds in position. For variation and depth, both the top and bottom faces of the fronds are exposed. The anthurium's heart-shaped, plastic-textured spathe, which dots the length of the center-piece, provides contrast in shape and color. The theme is extended to the place settings.

TROPICAL COILS

Taking their cue from the coconut leaf baskets woven throughout tropical countries to hold temple offerings or to steam food, coiled coconut or other fronds can make inexpensive but attractive centerpieces. The fronds are simply coiled around the hand to achieve the desired diameter and placed upright in a suitable container. Alternatively, leaves may be scored and folded, then placed in simple box frames to form innovative "floral nests". Any flexible, elongated leaf is suitable. The natural spring in each will hold the structure in position. For maximum impact, contrasting or toning flowers can be tucked within the interlocking form or placed on top of flatter coils.

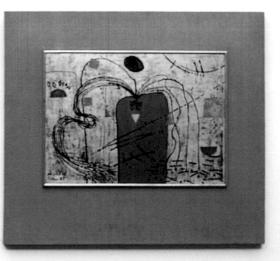

Left: Rainbow tree leaves are turned on their sides and coiled to highlight their richly colored borders. The pinkish-orange petals of the ascocenda further ignite the palette.

Right: The tapered lines of coconut fronds add a rippled effect to this loosely coiled candle arrangement. Miniature cattleya blossoms and ascocenda balance on the coconut ridges, their stems just skimming the surface of the water below.

Below right: Powerful lime green cattleyas, with their trademark splash of purple, emerge from nests of interwoven coconut fronds held in place by teakwood frames.

DEFINING LINES

Whether in the wild or in garden settings, leaves are usually viewed en masse. However, when order is applied and leaves become vessels as well as complementary foliage, their true beauty can be revealed. Single leaves may be folded at intervals and positioned in vases to produce an airy but angular, three-dimensional effect. Trimmed leaves may be turned on their sides and packed into simple frames. Color variations within the leaves, whether a vibrant lime center or a reverse scheme, highlight the line of the leaves and contribute to the geometry of these exciting new forms. Attention is also focused on the intriguing texture of the tropical leaves. Flowers are used sparingly to add final flair.

Left: Striking pandanus fronds form a natural platform for suspending a miniature cattleya stem over a water-filled vessel. The two-tone greenery is a refreshing addition to the high-gloss surroundings.

Right: A mauve-pink miniature cattleya lends intimacy and warmth to this metallic and glass interior. Fastened to a bamboo skewer for height, it is given center billing among the folded greenery.

Above: Trimmed snake plant leaves, also known as mother-in-law's tongue, are inserted into an iron frame. Pale porcelain flowers, a member of the hoya genus, emerge from the loose arrangement, much like budding creepers on a garden fence. Water-filled vials behind the leaves feed each stem.

Right: Parallel fins of fleshy spider lily leaves stand upright, wedged into square teak boxes. The natural shape and color variation of each leaf create a dynamic play of line and depth, while the dainty ixora blossom, most often seen in its natural ball-like cluster, adds its own exclamation mark.

LYRICAL LEAFWORK

When playing with a blade of grass or a coconut frond, there is a natural tendency to explore the form's potential, either by twisting it around the wrist or simply holding a loop in place. The shape of the leaf retracts as soon as it is released. The natural spring of such leaves can be harnessed to create lively and original floral displays. Mimicking the natural sway of palms, blooms may be threaded on to the flexible spines of the coconut frond, through looped coconut leaves, and inserted into lengths of banana trunk. The flowers will appear to dance on their supporting greenery, adding an air of frivolity to the arrangement. In whimsical as well as practical displays, looped leaves may also be used to support their floral subjects above wide-necked vases.

Left: Looped fronds elevate pink anthuriums above a monochromatic collection of ceramic vessels. The fronds both maintain the gentle arc of each stem and reinforce the individual charm of the containers.

Right: Coconut fronds looped beneath the hanging petals of the spider lily create an airy centerpiece in the home of Prasert and Sunathee Isvarphornchai that allows the free flow of dinner party conversation. The refreshing white-on-green color scheme is echoed in the lengths of banana tree trunk lining the base of the table arrangement.

LIVING SCULPTURES

The waxy lotus leaf is an ideal wrapping material while the banana leaf is frequently used for cooking and food presentation. Freestanding panels covered in these durable leaves form an unusual floral canvas that highlights the inherent form and line of each species. The careful positioning of lotus blossoms and seeds on the vertical plane leads the eye downwards, much as if reading a scroll. To create these "exhibition" stands, leaves are first attached to a wooden block and then inserted into the supporting metal frame. As the ageing process creeps across the arrangement, and the color and texture of the foliage are transformed, another exciting visual dimension is added to each "living sculpture".

Opposite: Freestanding banana leaf panels flank heirloom calligraphy on a landing in the home of Viboon Techakalayatum and Velvadi Sritrairatana, forming an original but reverent celebration of nature.

Left: The pale undersides of lotus leaves are gently fanned along the length of the freestanding panels and dotted with lotus buds. The natural lines of the leaves mimic the ripples of a pond and provide an interesting contrast to the adjacent, more geometric and deeper hued banana leaf and lotus seed arrangement.

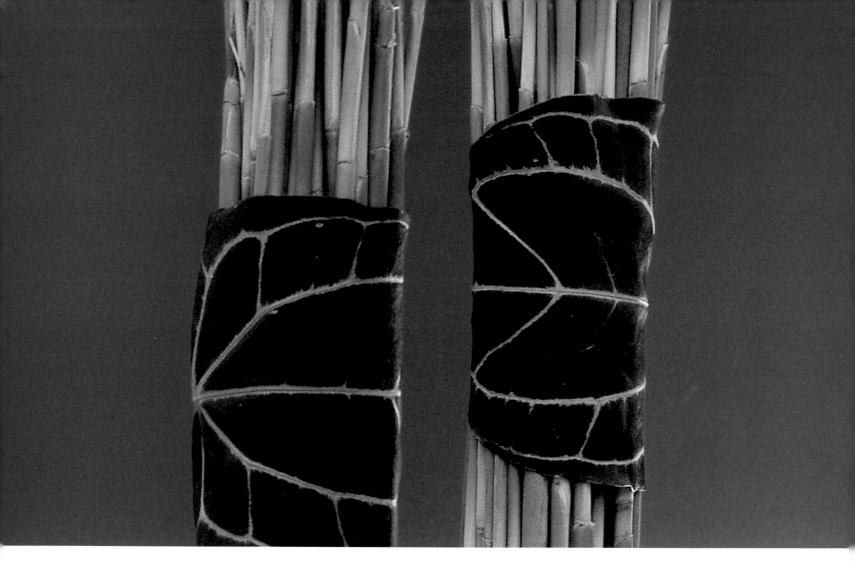

STEM SUPPORT

A symbol of longevity in the Chinese culture, and a favorite subject of artists, bamboo has long been transformed into a myriad of practical items and put to use in thousands of different ways around the world. Available in many lengths, diameters and colors, this fast-growing tree-like grass, with its strong, woody, hollow stems and ringed joints, continues to capture the modern imagination. Both the emotive and functional characteristics of bamboo can be incorporated into floral design. Used in combination with other tropical stems, such as horsetail and plants of the costus family, bamboo can lend not only structural support to a floral arrangement but also inject a feeling of classic Oriental balance, order and harmony.

NATURAL SCAFFOLDS

The scale may differ but the principle remains the same when bamboo scaffolding, an enduring feature of many building sites in Asia, is brought inside and used as a support for tropical floral arrangements. This all-natural structure, free of joining materials, effortlessly secures larger stems in position while capturing the essence of the bloom. It firmly places the emphasis on the striking shapes and colors of the flowers it supports. The tensile strength of bamboo can also be transformed into an alluring display when used as a domed cage over a fragile blossom. The subject within is enveloped in an air of mystique as bamboo reinvents itself yet again.

Left and right: Stripped of their supporting greenery, bold yellow and red bracts of *Heliconia caribeae* are a dramatic and undeniably tropical addition to Raymond Eaton's spacious Bangkok home. *Heliconia caribeae*, which grows up to a height of 20 feet, can be scaled to suit the setting. The deceptively strong but flexible golden bamboo lattice at the base of the acrylic containers secures the carnival-like forms in position without competing with their performance.

Left: Originating in the Caribbean Islands, *Heliconia caribeae* is one of several hundred species of this beautiful, exotic plant. It is also deceptive. The colorful red, yellow and orange bracts are merely a protective covering for the relatively insignificant flowers that are housed within.

Above: Golden bamboo forms a protective cage over this eye-catching floating hibiscus and heightens its perceived value. The common tropical flower becomes a small organic treasure set amidst stainless steel and glass while the green stripes on the bamboo mimic the surrounding reflections.

Surrounded by the bold, primary palette of this interior, an elegant arrangement uses form rather than color to make a statement. Horsetail stems are connected by bamboo skewers to form functional yet attractive platforms that prevent the white curcuma flowers from falling into the vases below.

SUPPORTING STEMS

When searching for greenery to frame a floral arrangement, leaves are usually the first choice. However, tropical stems – the nutrient thoroughfare and lifeline of a plant – should also be considered. Stems can quickly and easily be transformed into innovative supporting structures with a contemporary look and feel. Because of their exotic, eye-catching beauty, many tropical blooms need little else to enhance their breathtaking colors and shapes than a structure of stems. Construction is simple and intuitive. If stems are too short for a vessel, horsetail "platforms" can be used to suspend the blossoms just below the waterline, preventing them from sinking into elongated vases. Stems from the costus family can be placed along the length of a dining table, creating a dramatic backdrop for the rich tones of the flame tree or similarly spectacular blooms. The same flowing lines replicated in a vertical column can also form a practical display that is easy to maintain. Stems by themselves, free of flowers and in varying shades of green, can also be refreshing. As with all scaffolding solutions, the floral subjects can be swiftly rearranged according to mood and occasion.

Above and right: Crown of thorn blooms are considered lucky in Thailand where they are common verandah plants along the city's many canals. Here they are supported on a variegated platform of Belgian evergreen stems. Pins secure each lattice in position.

A collection of containers filled with stems and leaves of varying heights, shades and textures creates an indoor garden. For added visual interest, the glassware also differs. The overall effect is quick and simple to achieve. Different plants are placed in different vessels and arranged in a location filled with light. Maintenance is minimal. Some stems, like the bamboo, will last longer than others and need only be replenished occasionally.

Stainless steel cylinders anchor
lengths of reeds in this fuschia-
colored alcove. Yellow miniature
cattleyas held in position by the
reeds climb towards the decorative anthurium leaf binding.
Noted for their velvety texture,
the anthurium leaves are the
key to maintaining the soaring
height of both columns.

Left: The dynamic form and rich color of flame tree blossoms create lively and seasonal focal points on an elevated raft of costus stems. The horizontal line and palette of the arrangement harmonize with the room's refined lines and strong perspective.

Below: In this variation of the arrangement, Barbados pride flowers appear to flow through perspex gates on a lush bed of snake grass stems.

Left: Segments of golden bamboo held horizontally in a simple U-shaped metallic frame provide a rustic and understated platform for pride of India blooms. Also known as the rose of India, the flower is a delicate contrast to the bold surroundings.

Right: A freestanding "forest" of golden bamboo with differing diameters rises from a water-lined tray. Opulent lavender pride of India sprays emerge from holes drilled into the sides of the bamboo, allowing the blooms to drink from the tray.

FLUTED FRAMES

A grove of bamboo can be likened to a one-stop shop for home building projects. Soaring trunks become the framework of an entire house as well as fences, gates and screens. Woven panels become the walls. Bamboo is also the chosen material for household items such as knives, skewers, fasteners, fish traps and water pipes. Adding the final floral touch, bamboo in its simplest form becomes an effective display tool for tropical blooms. Free of intricate joinery, standardized lengths can be wedged into metallic frames just wide enough for a snug fit. Flowers can then be positioned between the trunks rather than inside and the entire arrangement positioned vertically in smaller spaces or horizontally on tables and shelves.

Left: Upright but slightly irregular lengths of sugar cane complement the wooden tones and horizontal lines in this bathroom. Frangipani blooms wedged between the cane add welcome curves, subtle color and heady fragrance.

Above: Reversing natural order, yellow saraca flowers trim the bases of these twin arrangements. Mesh hidden within the ceramic containers supports the rare black bamboo branches, which in turn support the floral rims.

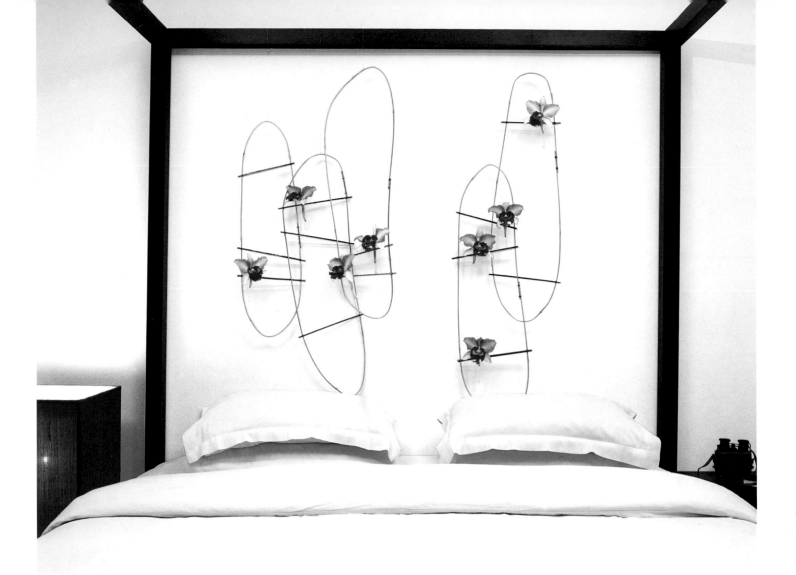

IN SUSPENSE

Split bamboo fashioned into pendant sculptures challenges traditional vase arrangements and maximizes the beauty of weeping blooms. Whether shaped into a circular floral curtain or a ladder-like structure, the flexibility and tensile strength of bamboo is the key. Neatly wound copper wire is used to secure circular shapes as well as the cross bracing of larger structures. The flowers can be attached in one of two ways depending on their form. Naturally hanging sprays are simply inserted into tiny water vials fastened to each frame. Individual blossoms are positioned between parallel strips of bamboo bound together at either end. The natural spring in the material keeps the flowers in position.

Above: Five irregularly shaped bamboo "scaffolds", suspended from the frame of this bed, infuse a modern twist into the canopy concept without cluttering the spare interior. Bamboo cross bracing holds the deep pink cattleyas in position.

Opposite: Strips of bamboo fastened by copper wire make an attractive installation on a plain wall. Lime cattleyas, easily replaced, are inserted between the cross bracing.

Thailand's national flower, the golden shower, covers trees in a sea of yellow when in bloom in late February and March. Reflecting the flower's natural fall, this suspended installation is Buddhist inspired. It symbolizes the cycles of life and souls working their way from one world to another. Thin strips of bamboo are fashioned into rings of varying sizes and then suspended in an overlapping but light and spacious arrangement. The tiny, translucent vials of water sustaining the delicate blooms are barely noticeable.

CRAFT CREATIONS

The story behind a handcrafted item can often be as fascinating as the form itself. Deceptively simple objects can belie centuries of practice, passed from one generation to the next. The purchasing experience may hold a host of memories and stories waiting to be shared. Souvenirs rescued from the isolation of a cupboard shelf can be put to creative use in floral arrangements. Cattleyas sprinkled across a bamboo flute or a frangipani resting in a coconut ladle provide fresh interpretations of both objects. The simplicity of freshly picked floral tokens set against the rustic charm of a handmade item will undoubtedly generate renewed interest in the distant but original context and will also invite the curiosity of guests.

TRADITIONAL TONES

The richly detailed patterns and intricate techniques of indigenous handicrafts offer a perfect foil to the exquisite and ephemeral nature of tropical blooms. Rather than restrict such items to the role for which they were intended, explore their use in modern floral applications. Monochromatic arrangements with one or two blooms that celebrate the flower's natural beauty and perhaps evoke a seasonal change can make a sensuous focal point in any room. A subdued split bamboo container will enhance the warm, rich tones emanating from a boldly colored flower. Woven fans, mirroring the original shape of the palm leaf, though in a softer palette, can form a quiet background for an understated bloom. Arrangements may also be placed on lacquer or wooden trays to contrast or complement the flowers' texture and tones.

Opposite: Cattleyas, reminiscent of details on a richly embroidered silk hanging, are inserted into acrylic sheeting.

Below left: Voluptuous cattleyas nestle in a varnished split bamboo flower basket.

Below right: An amazon lily resting atop a dried palm leaf fan makes a simple but practical floral offering.

INSPIRED ORBITS

The Asian game of *takraw*, in which two teams of youths keep a woven rattan ball in play across a high net using anything but their hands, provides unexpected inspiration for tropical floral displays. A cluster of the tightly woven balls in a wooden tray, sprinkled with fuschia-colored orchids, creates a spirited conversation piece. The arrangement can be placed either on a floor or table. Larger, simplified versions of the ball, with a looser weave, can be grouped to form dynamic "installations". Spheres of rattan forming protective cages around flowers which peep coyly from within can bring a hint of magic to any interior. Hardy blooms are recommended for these water-free arrangements.

Left and right: A feminine slant is given to the traditionally masculine game of *takraw* in this charming floor arrangement. The rich pink and yellow hues of ascocenda (left) and cattleya blossoms (right) sprinkled on both original and decorative versions of the *takraw* ball are set against the warm tones of the rattan and the darker wood of the roughly hewn tray. The varying sizes of the balls and the weaves add depth to this playful composition.

Bamboo painted black and dotted with white dendrobiums encircles a candle within a simple glass globe. As if attracted to the flame, a moth orchid floats beneath the candle. The water adds further reflections to the delicate play of light.

A path of floral lanterns leading down the stairs and to the front door signals the beginning of a magical evening. Cinderella's slippers await. Flickering shadows line the walls, adding to the ambience. Providing a fresh twist to an old concept, these bamboo lanterns can also be arranged down the length of a dining table, along a sideboard, around an outdoor pool or used to guide guests through a garden and into the home.

WOVEN BLOOMS

The elaborate festivals and ceremonies which play such a large part in the lives of Asian peoples are a rich source of inspiration for floral design. The *som dok* is an offering flower woven from bamboo and used in northern Thai culture (formerly known as Lanna), where festivals with decorative banners, flowers and candles dot the yearly calendar. The radiating tips of the *som dok*, a lasting and reusable item, are decorated with tiny jasmine flowers. Here the *som dok* is reinterpreted for a contemporary space. Its rustic palette complements modern interiors, especially if used in combination with supporting bases formed of natural materials, such as sections of water hyacinth stems and banana trunk.

Left: Woven bamboo flower forks (*som dok*), their radiating points tipped with white crown flowers, stand to attention on a raft of sliced banana trunk. Viewed from above, the forks form a light and delicate mass.

Right: Paper gardenia buds are attached to *som dok* to create this tiered arrangement. Closely stacked water hyacinth stems encased in rectangular perspex containers provide a base for the forks. The mirror behind magnifies the delicate profiles of the floral forks.

FLORAL LANTERNS

The versatility of bamboo provides endless possibilities for floral art. Two strips of split bamboo, looped into circles and joined by fine copper wire, can form simple floral cradles for both bold specimens and daintier blooms that are often seen only in clusters. The technique can be adapted to vessels of varying shapes and sizes and allows blooms to be positioned within as desired. Shorter stemmed flowers can rest on the waterline while longer stems can be suspended above in their own hanging baskets. Staggering blooms at different heights and spreading their color across an array of translucent glassware will add something special to any interior.

In this floral arrangement, simplified bamboo balls are gently eased into rectangular glass containers. The long stems of the red miniature cattleyas reaching down to the water resemble small hanging lanterns. The color of the flowers accentuates the intricate detail of the ornate brocade *obi* spread out below.

METALLIC ACCENTS

Taming the vivid and varied forms of heliconias and other long-stemmed tropical flowers calls for special containers as well as sensitivity to scale, proportion and space. Metallic frames are an innovative alternative to tall vases, providing secure anchorage and allowing the foliage to fall as it would in its natural setting. The hard, cold permanence of metal also offers a stark tactile and visual contrast to the short-lived brilliance of tropical flowers. Stems become an extension of simple tubular grids or prisms. Flowers are suspended from above or ensnared within delicate web-like constructions. In large spaces, freestanding floral displays take on the function of a sculpture, to be viewed and wondered at from every angle.

METAL SUPPORT

Innovative metallic bases can be functional as well as aesthetically pleasing, breathing vitality into an arrangement of bold plant material. Space is the key. A design needs to be in proportion to its surroundings. Tiered configurations project soaring height while a series of standardized metal components creates a unified but spacious split-level installation. Flowers may be suspended within the clearly defined boundaries of a supporting prism. The overall effect is of movement and space as flowers are freed from the confines of a vase. Water, where it is needed, is subtly introduced into the shallow stainless steel trays lining the metal bases.

Left and right: A "pathway" of Egyptian papyrus supported by custom-made galvanized iron bases forms an enchanting transition to the upper levels of portrait artist Sakwut Wisesmanee's home. Slim green candles inserted into alternate bases blend with the surrounding stems, reminiscent of fireflies on a tropical evening. The stems arranged up the stairs add height and contribute to the interesting perspective of the arrangement when viewed from the landing above.

Left: Cyclanthus leaves arch out of a metallic base in effortless symmetry to frame the *Heliconia orthotricha* cv. She. The vibrant bract is framed by foliage, much as it would appear in its natural setting.

Right: Reed mace, tuberoses and a base of floating lotuses are all held in position by an elevated grid, creating a delicate play of line, space and proportion. The metallic base adds symmetry to the arrangement without constricting the natural sway of the foliage.

The five-tiered structure of this commissioned installation in the lobby of The Sukhothai Bangkok symbolizes the five basic precepts of Buddhism. At once towering and light, the muted arrangement appears to float on its watery base.

Left: Sakul Intakul-designed tabletop vessels host contemplative lotus blossoms. The exposed stems reach down to drink from the shallow trays of water below. The petals are folded in geometric precision to prevent bruising of the open flowers as well as to expose their delicate inner beauty.

Below: Plump floating lotus blossoms crowned with lit candles contrast with the soaring lean lines of the tuberoses and spears of reed mace above.

Left: The unusual polished patina of rare black bamboo takes on an almost metallic form against a gold lacquer screen. The stems of the tuberoses attached to one of the curving metal supports are reflected in the granite flooring below.

Right: A mesh of taut brass strands gives internal geometry to a steel prism finished with a dull gold coating. The aquatic backdrop contributes to the optical illusion of "trapped" cattleyas dancing in a shimmering web. Cattleya blooms are tied to each supporting strand.

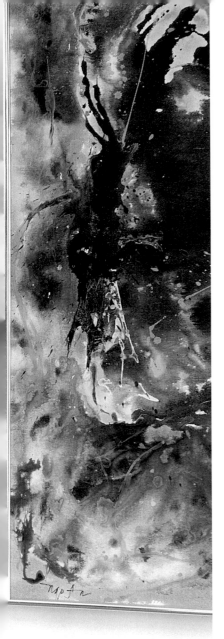

TUBULAR EXTENSIONS

Whether store bought or custom designed, simple metal tubing, cut to size and grouped together, gives floral designs a contemporary, graphic feel while offering firm support. Metal appears to bloom and stems become extensions of their shiny bases. Surprising scale is achieved given the size of the supports: towering bamboo trunks or reeds rise from small but stable floral-trimmed bases. Suspended pendants form elegant top–down "installations". Water supplies are subtly integrated into the displays. Stems are either inserted into tiny water vials attached to metallic prongs, or shallow, water-filled trays provide sustenance from below.

Left: A grid of steel tubes loosely packed in a metal container supports a tall column of reeds and a mass of shorter-stemmed curcuma bracts positioned around the base of their stems.

Opposite: Soaring twin columns of reed mace frame this doorway on the upper level of Raymond Eaton's home. Wild and refreshing spirals of *ylang-ylang* flowers encircle the base.

Left: In this eye-catching corner display, the delicate, fleeting beauty of flame tree blossoms individually placed in a custom-made tubular metal support provides a perfect counterpoise to the sturdy bamboo trunks.

Right: The ubiquitous hibiscus is given a fresh interpretation as a vivid trim at the base of this golden bamboo "grove". The frivolity of the flower's delicate petals and protruding stamens offsets the austerity of the bamboo trunks.

Left: A metal frame creates a support for green bamboo stems but does not inhibit their search for light in the void above. The vibrant green anthuriums at the base of the arrangement evoke the emergence of fresh bamboo shoots.

Top right: This spider lily's "web", interspersed with lime-colored buds, extends over a meandering grid of geometric steel. The overall effect is of flowering metal stems fed by a water-filled tray.

Below right: Water hyacinth stems form a supporting "hedge" for white hibiscus flowers. The circular tips of the sliced stems introduce a third element into the arrangement.

A bold black and white grid of herald's trumpet flowers on metallic stems is softened by the subtle shades of lime in the center of the flowers. The waxy petals offer an organic contrast to the metal stand and the marble and glass interior.

Sakul Intakul bronze "mangrove" pods house solitary ascocenda orchids in tiny water receptacles. Hung en masse at varying lengths and interspersed with the occasional empty container, they create an elegant "chandelier" effect.

WIRED WEBS

Spider webs are often felt before they are seen and continue to evade the eye even after being pointed out. The amazing detail and tensile strength of these geometric filament constructions, which often appear overnight and span seemingly impossible distances, can be replicated in floral arrangements. Nylon, mesh, chicken wire and steel frames can replace the spider's silk, either "ensnaring" prized blooms or supporting heavier stems such as the elephant ear plant and bracts of the heliconia. From a distance, flora will appear to float, barely contained by the surrounding metalwork. The glint of the artificial frames will, however, be revealed from certain angles, further mimicking the spider web.

Left: The broad leaves of the elephant ear plant form an inverted tripod within a taut web of nylon. Despite their weight, they barely touch the cubic metal frame because of the traction of the water-filled tray lined with chicken wire.

Opposite: The pendant blooms of *Heliconia chartacea* cv. Sexy Pink fall as they would in a garden setting. Native to the region between Guyana and Peru, their exotic lines and color are diffused within a series of stacked metallic cubes, creating a refreshing and spacious display.

Above: In this airy display, *Heliconia densiflora* cv. Fire Flash stems emerge from water-filled, mesh-covered trays as a three-layered "hedge": a silver netting cage gives way to lush greenery capped with a fiery rim.

Right: A trio of exquisite anthuriums appears to be free-standing in interconnected mesh spheres – a suitably sculptural setting for an exotic species. Natural back lighting silhouettes the fine wire base, enhancing the arrangement.

Left and right: Freestanding towers of reed mace and lotus blooms turn images of tranquil tropical ponds literally on their side. Crisp order, parallel lines and refined color replace wilful, entangled pond blossoms. This controlled interpretation harmonizes with the strict geometry of the space. Each reed mace stem and folded lotus is separated and cleaned before being inserted, one at a time, into the mesh grid.

DIVIDED ATTENTION

It is tempting to buy in bulk and arrive home laden with cut flowers ready to disperse liberally around the home. Certain occasions – and budgets – may, however, call for alternative solutions. A single spray in a vase, surrounded by a collection of empty containers, can form a casual and understated display. Separating blooms and dispersing their color across a number of identical containers can result in an effortless and rhythmic arrangement equally suited to a formal dining setting or as the focal point on a coffee table. Regardless of quantity, clever floral distribution can enhance a space with a measured and confident air. Each floral element, framed by a supporting vessel, becomes a centerpiece in its own right.

STUNNING SINGLES

In order to appreciate the singular beauty of many flowers, closer attention is required. Separating a floral arrangement into individual containers gives the eye a chance to explore the hues and textures of each isolated blossom. Differing heights and odd numbers are key to maintaining visual interest, while the repetition of shape and color conveys a sense of order. It is best to keep things simple, with one type of flower or foliage. The arrangements can be adapted to different scales, whether they are spread down the length of a dining table or arrayed along a sideboard. Containers, such as the specially designed Sakul Intakul vessels shown here, should be chosen to complement the color, shape and texture of each flower.

Right: A single spray of the oncidium orchid emerges from an eclectic display of glassware on a restored chest of drawers.

Opposite: Porcelain Sakul Intakul "tamarind" vases, each one housing a single elephant creeper bloom or its rolled leaf, snake their way through this casual breakfast setting.

Next page: Coral-colored anthuriums appear to sway on impossibly thin stems, evoking images of an underwater scene. The fluid forms are, however, firmly grounded in handmade ceramic oil lamps.

Left: Petite vanda orchids form decorative anchors to the sweeping line of each pandanus leaf.

Above left: Capturing the elegant lines of pale musseanda decorative leaves, bronze Sakul Intakul "tripods" throw delicate shadows on the timber flooring.

Above right: A brilliant velvet-petalled cattleya basks in reflected glory on red Japanese lacquerware.

Left: A trail of cymbidiums meanders across a tonal array of bronze Sakul Intakul vessels inspired by the shape of the starfruit. Nearby, a ceramic bowl replaces the original pod housing the seeds of the *Entada spiralis* creeper.

Above: In this warm coffee table arrangement, a green miniature cattleya sprouts from the grooves of a bronze Sakul Intakul vessel cast in the shape of a "pong pong" seed. Its organic inspiration is clustered on an adjacent ceramic tray.

ECLECTIC ELEGANCE

The sculptural qualities of tall tropicals are highlighted when one or two blooms are placed against muted and uncluttered backdrops. Vases can be used to create or reinforce an eclectic ambience, as shown in the work of Thai artist Thaiwijit Puengkasemsomboon who transforms humble junkyard objects into highly individual containers. For shorter stems or more common flowers, grouping is the key. Unified floral clusters may mingle with an assortment of other flowers and vessels. Prized vases may sit alongside recycled bottles. Drinking glasses can mimic the shape of larger neighbors. Weeds may complement precious blooms. Unexpected couplings will lead to distinctive displays.

Left: Nature merges into art as two exotic bird of paradise stems arc out of an equally fanciful junkyard sculpture, adding a touch of whimsy to a well-used filing cabinet. The adjacent lamp is also fashioned from salvaged items.

Opposite: Pink ginger bracts are surreal extensions to Thaiwijit Puengkasemsomboon's sideboard sculpture of found objects. Desert roses in a daffodil yellow salad bowl draw the eye to the foreground.

Right: Wispy green rhipsalis, a free-branching cactus, emerges from the twin openings of a ceramic vessel and inches its way across a filmy background in this soothing white-on-white setting.

Opposite: A lone coral tree branch, encircled by a sprinkling of its own foliage, is a refreshing addition to this muted bathroom. The arc of the stem complements the curvilinear glass container.

Top left: Green *ylang-ylang* flowers spiral out of Sakul Intakul disc-shaped "pods", adding a dash of lime to an afternoon tea setting.

Below left: A lady's slipper orchid adds a welcome flash of color to this green and white assembly of jasmine, crown flowers and spider lilies set on a low wooden table.

Clusters of *Monochoria hastata* and a single richly perfumed amaryllis lily stand tall amidst a grouping of glass bottles and containers. Old jars are placed beside prized glassware. Some are left empty to add breathing space and variety to the floral arrangement. Twine ties ensure the tall stems remain upright in the relatively low containers.

MASS APPEAL

Tropical flower markets offer a mass of color and intriguing varieties. Woven bamboo baskets brim with luxuriant petals and fragrant garlands perfume the scene, while the shoppers' arms soon fill with spontaneous purchases. Once home, finding the right vase to house your purchases may require some adaptation. Search the kitchen cupboards for containers; saucepans, crockery and bottles all offer potential. If the right size cannot be found, distribute the flowers across a cluster of vessels. They will retain their impact and the containers will add creative flair. No flower is too precious and no container too plain to be used. Importing this sense of color and vitality into the home may evoke memories of a distant sojourn or provide a contemporary interpretation of local heritage.

COLORFUL CLUSTERS

Filling a single large container – or a series of matching containers – with a mass of identical blooms conveys a sense of abundance and is a wonderful celebration of the color and fecundity of the tropics. Variations in the size and height of massed arrangements add both interest and impact. A dome of mesh can be stretched across broad-necked containers and stems inserted to create lush floral coverings. The same method may be applied to small timber frames for mounted wall displays. Meanwhile, a cluster of tall plants such as the heliconia will act as a perfect counterpoise to the weight and majesty of heavy ceramic urns.

Left: Barely contained by their plump pink petals, lotuses offer an ephemeral beauty that lasts for only a day or two. They are a contrast to the more permanent treasures on display.

Right: Lush crowns of lotuses emerge from shallow, hand-beaten steel bowls in Ou Baholyodhin's living room. The voluptuous forms burst open to reveal a glimpse of their textured cores surrounded by a froth of pinkish-white stamens.

Top left: Pink ixora and blooming *Bauhinia winitii* nestle among a collection of hand-thrown vessels. The lack of symmetry in the flowers parallels the eclectic nature of the craft items on display.

Below left: Rich tufts of red ixora in a large ceramic bowl add color and drama to an austere concrete stairwell. Commonly called jungle flame or jungle geranium, the plant's tiny flowers, packed into dense, ball-like clusters, are ideal for massed arrangements.

Right: Twin ixora clusters provide a bold injection of color amidst the treasured finds and salvaged floorboards of Thaiwijit Puengkasesomboon's home.

Vibrant primary colors paired with softer pastel shades make for a carefree rooftop setting. Fuschia-colored chain of love flowers, also known as the Mexican creeper, froth out of a fire engine red enamel pot, adding to the air of frivolity.

A riotous mass of multicolored miniature cymbidium hybrids spread across four different containers makes a cheerful and harmonious display. The glassware, of different heights and shapes, echoes the dominant citrus tones of the flowers.

Fiery Okinawa torch bracts form a vivid focal point among the atmospheric blues cloaking the entranceway of Thaiwijit Puengkasemsomboon's home. A decorative variety of the banana family, the bracts stand tall in a hand-painted ceramic urn by fellow artist Chakrawich Pongsittipol. The stems are loosely tied with twine to keep them upright.

A large earthen water jar provides sturdy support for a mass of bold, interlocking heliconia bracts backed by a fan of reed mace stems. Its smaller neighbor contains finer, hot pink-tipped *Heliconia psittacorum* cv. Sassy.

Left and right: A water-free parade of color floats across a scrolled teak coffee table in the Isvarphornchai home. It is a novel alternative to a single, formal display. The rows of variegated graptophyllum and pastel flower leaves are intersected by a bold stripe of paper-thin bougainvillea bract. The foliage is simply folded into the individual glass tubes where it unfoils to hug the inner surface. The same effect can be achieved using a collection of drinking glasses.

Floral art takes to the wall in the home of Sakwut Wisesmanee. Plush squares of scarlet cock's comb flowers are displayed vertically in mesh-lined teak boxes. The boxed flowers form tactile, organic fixtures, in lively juxtaposition to the size and color of the heavier frame on the adjacent wall. Whenever necessary, the boxes can be replenished with fresh blooms.

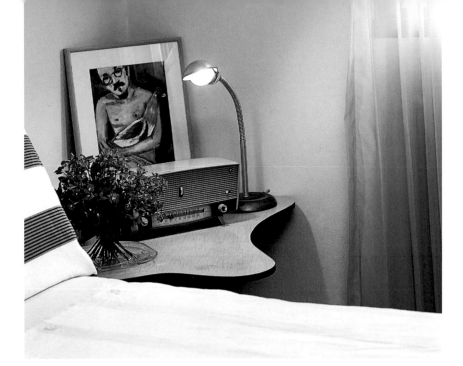

Left: The soothing lavender hues of Philippine violets offer bedside calm. Fastened mid-stem, they stand upright in a shallow pool of water on a simple glass plate.

Below: A rectangular steel vessel filled with pale musse-anda decorative leaves infuses delicate line and color into a controlled, geometric interior.

NATURAL WRAPS

Tropical foliage can do much more than support flowers or provide color and textural contrast to a floral arrangement. In the spirit of merging interior and exterior
boundaries, it can be used to stunning effect to decorate the outside of containers,
enriching an overall arrangement. Ever versatile, foliage can quickly transform and
add aesthetic value to ordinary and often overlooked household items, such as
plastic containers, tins and glassware. Sliced banana trunk and segments of bamboo are ideal for encasing larger vessels, while leaves wrapped around standard
glassware will unify a table setting. The chosen foliage needs to be reasonably
durable and should suit the size of the container. It can be fixed in place with twine
or double-sided tape. The color of the foliage, which should complement rather
than overwhelm the flowers above, can be changed to suit the occasion.

Left: A spiked mass of crimson
Heliconia psittacorum cv.
Lady Di, held within a square-
shaped base, forms an attractive
and durable outdoor centerpiece. Small segments of
golden bamboo are wrapped
around the container and
fastened in place with twine.

Opposite: Low-slung furniture
beckons on interior designer
Niki Frei's terrace. Vivid heliconia
claws climb out of an adjacent
bamboo-trimmed vessel.

Above and below right: This charming table setting for four is dappled with purple vandas. The individual blooms, resting atop humble tumblers wrapped in calathea leaves, blend harmoniously with the crackled glaze of the crockery.

Left: Sheer sari curtains soften the tropical glare and form a light and airy backdrop to a sideboard display. This color scheme is a reversal of the main table display below. The circular petals of lime vanda orchids rest on the rims of glassware wrapped in *Calathea* leaves, their purple undersides exposed.

Pink orchid tree flowers are poised above a grid of tall, rectangular glass containers. Tricolored leaves from the rainbow tree lend their geometric stripes to the exterior of each vase. Double-sided tape is used to fix the leaves in position.

In this variation on the theme, the rainbow tree's tricolored leaves are wrapped around bold glass spheres, mirroring the swirling lines of the pink orchid tree flowers. The glossy surface of the tabletop produces a subtle reflection.

Opposite: Yellow mandevilla blossoms are spread over three containers in this cheerful display. Each container is constructed from the lime-colored spines of banana leaves and tied with coconut fronds.

Left: Plump buttercup tree flowers emerge from a geometric pandanus-lined vessel. The striped leaves, triangular in section, are trimmed to size and then attached to the container with double-sided tape.

Below: Clusters of yellow-hued orchids harmonize with "rustic" containers wrapped in sheaths of banana trunk and secured with banana fibers.

Left: A container of vivid purple water lilies wrapped in a deep green banana leaf echoes the lavender and lime tones of Niki Frei's bedroom and contributes to its air of tranquility.

Above: Sumptuous cattleyas spill out of glasses encased in banana leaf jackets. Back lighting softens the impact of these intensely colored blooms.

DIVINE INSPIRATIONS

In the tropics, both people and the divine are the recipients of flowers. Tropical blooms and leaves not only play an integral role in everyday life but are also an essential component of ceremonies and festivals. In some societies, floral crowns and garlands are worn as accessories or offered in greeting. A woman may pick a frangipani or purchase strands of jasmine to place in her hair, or she may weave the same blooms into temple offerings. Leaves can also be transformed into offering baskets. Inspiration may be drawn from the many cultural associations found in both the day-to-day and ceremonial use of tropical flowers. A mood of contemplation as well as innovative synergy will be infused into home floral displays.

SYMBOLIC GESTURES

Conical arrangements, inspired by religious architecture and accoutrements and aided by the fascinating composition of tropical foliage, inject a feeling of nobility and drama into floral art. Floral "processions" and garland-inspired designs speak of both religious practices and daily life in the tropics. The imaginative application of foliage to freestanding columns and cubic installations can add a magical quality to contemporary interiors. Outdoors, vibrant totems and organic candle holders lend an air of mystique to both daytime and evening garden settings. Understated colors, simple shapes and delicate fragrances symbolize the pure and the divine.

Left: Spire-shaped vessels, seemingly made of ceramic are, in fact, fashioned from peelings of the fleshy trunk of the crinum lily. Scented *ylang-ylang* flowers add a crowning touch.

Right: An ethereal procession of banana leaf cones glides along a glass tabletop as if drawn to the light. Reflections magnify the water-free arrangement. Fragrant tuberoses add heightened sensory appeal to this contemporary interpretation of Thai religious offerings.

Left: Freestanding pillars covered with lotus leaves and tuberoses line a candlelit waterway in the lobby of the Dusit Hotel's Devarana Spa in Bangkok. Inspired by the *Tribhumphraruang,* an ancient Thai text, the overall effect is of an enchanted pathway leading to a heavenly garden pavilion.

Above: Tuberoses climbing up the lotus leaf covered pillars infuse the mystical ambience with their sweet perfume. The overlapping lotus leaf "scales" are attached to wire frame columns which are surprisingly light and easy to move.

Left: Lotus leaf-covered cubes tumble down an ornate staircase, creating a dramatic and kinetic installation.

Right: "Organic origami" transforms two-dimensional lotus leaves into cubic canvases for pale herald's trumpet blooms. The lotus leaves are stretched over wire frames, with their radiating spines emphasizing each corner of the cubes.

Opposite: Long strands of tiny crown flowers form an elegant and airy room divider.

Left: Given as a form of greeting, this Thai garland is woven from orange jessamine leaves and covered in a delicate net of tiny paper gardenias. A tassle of crown flowers is trimmed with mock rose buds that are also cleverly fashioned from orange jessamine leaves.

Below: Millions of crown flowers and jasmine buds are threaded daily by nimble-fingered vendors throughout Asia to form garlands and other religious offerings.

Above left: A pagoda-shaped floral float is made of seven tiers of banana trunk encased in its own leaf. Globe amaranth blossoms trim each tier.

Above right: A central metal prong secures each tier of this arrangement in place.

Right: A gustavia blossom forms a focal point for devotion in front of this spirit house by artist Doytibetra Duchanee.

Left: Slices of banana trunk
attached to jade-colored
banana columns with bamboo
skewers support lit candles
in fashion designer Nagara
Sambandaraksa's garden.
Skewered frangipani blooms
spiral up the organic pillars.

Above: Gustavia blossoms form
reverent offerings before a
sculpture of Buddha's footprint.
Each flower rests on squares
of banana trunk that are covered
in banana leaves and fastened
with bamboo staples.

Visible from the garden, a group of oranges, symbolic of wealth in the Chinese culture, is proudly displayed atop a carved wooden seat in this vestibule. Individually bound in bamboo leaves, a symbol of longevity, and adorned with desert rose blooms, the arrangement is a modern twist on Chinese New Year house gifts. Parcels of the fruit are usually presented to hosts to wish them prosperity during the coming year.

Vibrant orange contrasts with striking green in this dynamic cluster. The exquisite desert roses on top of the arrangement not only add festive cheer but also connote the color red, a symbol of prosperity and fertility in the Chinese culture.

Right: Distinct seasonal change is rarely apparent in the tropics, though subtle changes do occur. Buttercup trees flower only in the dry season while the leaves of the sea almond tree turn to red and fall twice a year.

Below: Autumn-toned totems made from sea almond leaves and buttercup tree flowers stand in colorful contrast to Thai artist Doytibetra Duch-anee's "moonscape" sculpture of compressed aluminium cans.

Vivid garlands of marigolds, commonly used in north Indian ceremonies and weddings, have inspired these floral totems. The original color scheme has been adapted and refined for this outdoor setting. A central vertical metal prong replaces the needle and thread in the construction of the pillars. A painting by Thai artist and sculptor Doytibetra Duch-anee provides a luminous background to the totems.

PLANT DIRECTORY

Right: Caged pink orchid tree flowers infuse a shot of color into this monochromatic interior. Along with the elongated shape of the glass vase and the diffused light, they conspire to create a dynamic interpretation of the sandstone neighbor.

General Plant Care

A few simple tips can prolong the vase life of tropical flowers and foliage.

1. Clean all containers thoroughly before use to inhibit the growth of bacteria, particularly in steamy tropical countries.

2. Remove leaves that will sit below the water line. This reduces the amount of plant material that may decay and maintains the water quality.

3. Cut all stems on an angle immediately before inserting them into water to maximize the surface area for water absorption.

4. Replace container water, clean vessels, trim stems and remove wilted petals and foliage daily to preserve remaining flora.

Large submerged arrangements will, of course, be difficult to change on a daily basis so choose thick petalled flowers that will not bruise easily under water pressure.

Replenish small floating arrangements daily but allow larger installations to run their natural course.

Pick hardy flowers for water-free arrangements.

CREDITS

The authors and publisher would like to thank the location owners and designers who kindly opened their beautiful homes and premises, as well as those who loaned their products for photography.

Location Key
l = left, r = right, a = above, b = below

London-based Thai designer **Ou Baholyodhin**: pp. 28, 29, 42, 44, 45a, 54, 55, 64–6, 72–7, 79r, 80–5, 88–91, 93, 101, 120–2, 123r, 132, 134, 135

Raymond Eaton, businessman, collector and long-time resident of Thailand: pp. 1, 2, 4, 5, 7, 9–13, 16–23, 24b, 25, 40, 43, 45b, 46, 47, 56–63, 67–70, 102–6, 130a

Interior designer **Niki Frei**: pp. 50, 146–55

Prasert Isvarphornchai, businessman, and his airline executive wife **Sunathee**, and their interior designer **Panarin Manuyakorn**: pp. 14, 15, 27, 32, 51, 78, 87, 124, 133, 142, 143, 175

Artist **Thaiwijit Puengkasemsomboon** and his wife **Gade**: pp. 33, 79l, 118, 119, 126, 127, 129, 131, 133, 136a, 137–41, 145a, 165b

Fashion and textile designer **Nagara Sambandaraksa**: pp. 27, 86, 156, 157, 166–73

Interior designer **Viboon Techakalayatum** and his wife **Velvadi Sritrairatana**: pp. 6, 8, 30, 31, 41, 52, 53, 71, 100, 107a, 109, 114–16, 125, 128, 130b, 164

Portrait artist **Sakwut Wisesmanee**: pp. 48, 49, 92, 94–6, 110–13, 123l, 136b, 144, 145b, 176

Devarana Spa, The Dusit Thani Hotel, Bangkok: pp. 24a, 107b, 108, 158–63, 165a

The Sukhothai Bangkok, A Beaufort Hotel: pp. 26, 34–9, 97–9

Containers, Vessels and Props
Assembly Bangkok Co., Ltd.: Place mats p. 119, Vases p. 137.15 Yenakat Rd., Chongnontree, Yannawa, Bangkok 10120. Tel +66 2249 2046; Fax +66 2672 9857; E-mail info@assemblybkk.com; www.assemblybkk.com

Black Earth Pottery Studio: Ceramic oil lamps pp. 120–2. 613 M. 1, Pracha-uthit Rd., Bangmod, Tungkru, Bangkok 10140. Tel +66 1829 2722; Fax +66 2870 3402; E-mail blackearth_ben @yahoo.com

Cocoon Design Co., Ltd.: Crockery pp.148, 149b, Vases p. 50. 999 Gaysorn Plaza, 3rd Floor, Ploenchit Rd., Lumpini, Phatumvan, Bangkok 10330. Tel +66 2656 1006; Fax +66 2656 1007

Middle Ltd., Part.: Ceramic urn p. 140. 98 M. 4, T. Sanpapao, A. Sansai, Chiangmai 50210. Tel/Fax +66 5335 1269; E-mail middle@middle-middle.com

MöM Earth: Ceramic tea cups pp. 33, 136a. 54 Soi Praramkao 59, Praramkao Rd., Saunloung, Bangkok 10250. Tel/Fax +66 2732 1908; E-mail momearth@hotmail.com

Thaiwijit Puengkasemsomboon: Sculptural vases pp. 126, 127. 67/122 Amornpan 9, Soi Senanikom 1, Baholyodhin Rd., Ladprao, Bangkok

10230. Tel +66 2570 2090; E-mail thaiwijit @yahoo.com

Sakul Intakul Studio: Acrylic containers pp. 2, 9, 10–16, 24b, 43, 45a, 56–8, 62, 63, 67, 78, 87, Brass containers pp. 97–9, Bronze vessels pp. 32, 109, 117, 123l, 124, 125, 130a, Metal containers pp. 28–31, 48, 51, 66, 68–70, 92–6, 100–8, 110–15, 135, 145b, 172–3, Porcelain vessels p. 119, Wooden containers pp. 45b, 49, 52, 53, 144. 47 Soi Rajavithee 2, Samsennai, Phayathai, Bangkok 10400. Tel +66 2644 9439; Fax +66 2644 9437; E-mail sakulintakul@yahoo.com; www.sakulflowers.com

Other Assistance
The authors would also like to thank the following people for their valuable contributions to this project:

Yvan Van Outrive, M.L. Chiratorn Chirapravati, Wipawadee Sirimongkolkasem, Yaowanoot Soimora, Waltraud Waldner, Pornroj Angsanakul, Panarin Manuyakorn, Kamon Angkavichai, Surapat Chaiyongyos, Rungsima Kasikranund, Vichai Boo, Chalit Nakpawan and Chatchawan Pisitpaisankun

The **Sakul Flowers** team, for sourcing plant materials and props, and assisting with arrangements: Sombun Kringkrai, Amara Namsapanan, Sutat Komutmas, Anek Wasana, Orathai Hoitaku, Can Krasaetow, Rundon Saejew, Tee Bhokee and Somkid Honganurak.

The **Intakul family**, who have always given their complete support.